THE PRETTIEST GIRL AT THE DANCE

POEMS

JOHN DORSEY

BLUE HORSE PRESS   REDONDO BEACH, CALIFORNIA   2020

THE PRETTIEST GIRL AT THE DANCE

POEMS

JOHN DORSEY

Blue Horse Press
Redondo Beach,
California

Cover art: "Woman Overlooking a Rail Station,
Mußbach, Germany. 2013."
Blue Horse Press Archives ©
Used by permission

Editors: Jeffrey and Tobi Alfier
Blue Horse Press logo: Amy Lynn Alfier (1996)

ISBN 978-0-578-81878-8

This and other Blue Horse Press Titles may be found at
www.bluehorsepress.com

For Nikki Delamotte, in loving memory,
the prettiest girl in the afterlife

Acknowledgments

These poems were created with generous support from Osage Arts Community, many thanks are given to Mark McClane, Tony Hayden & the OAC Board.

Work included here has appeared or is forthcoming in *Turn A Phrase, Better Than Starbucks, Chiron Review, Glove, Live Nude Poems, Trampoline, Inefavel, The Rust Belt Review* and *Street Value*.

Contents

About the Author

Introduction

John Dorsey: Slicing Right Down to the Heart

Do you remember where you were 25 years ago in December? Sitting in a classroom daydreaming about the rich days to come, or maybe already years removed and punching a time clock in a small town that you had yet to find the courage to escape from?

I am certain that if you were to ask John that very question, he would have a precise answer for you.

John Dorsey has spent the last 25 years continuously sharpening and polishing his words for the page, much like you would sharpen and polish a dull handcrafted knife that you have just found half buried in the Pennsylvania dirt—beneath the discarded, ghostly appearance there are still pieces of soul from the man who birthed the blade; there are smeared fingerprints from all who have held the handle. John Dorsey knows this. His words are his knife blade.

He has scratched that blade against the concrete streets, sidewalks, and alleyways across this globe. He has wettened it with his own blood, sweat and tears. He has tied it to a string and tossed it into the ocean, into countless rivers, just to pull it out and hold it up to the moon. It has yet to have that desired consummate reflection from every angle, so the processes continue.

I wish I could say that I have known John for all those 25 years, however it was not until 2016 that John and I met through social media. He was a few months into an artist residency at the Osage Arts Community in Belle, Missouri, and I was living just a couple hours away in Carrollton.

We talked quite a few times and had even featured at some of the same reading events prior to the first road trip that we took together in October of that year. It was discovered during that drive to Toledo, that our traveling styles were nearly one in the same. It was a fantastic weekend that gave us many moments we still talk about to this day—The mysterious appearing underwear in a KFC parking lot story. The Peaches and Meat story. The Jason Baldinger and Scott Silsbe should have skipped Indianapolis and came to Toledo story. And of course, pretty girl stories.

Since that first trip, John and I have taken many more. We have traveled for poetry. We have traveled for weddings and anniversaries. We have traveled for nothing more than to visit dear friends across this country. Once, we drove through a tornado in Texas. We blew up a radiator in Chicago. We popped a tire on a highway pothole in Tennessee. One time, we overworked a transmission in Wyoming; it was there that we were left to stay in a hotel room with a half-star review and a broken heater.

Sure, all those last things may sound like horrible traveling stories, but if you know John like I know him, then you know that they were all rewarding moments. They were all opportunities for him to continue sharpening his blade.

One day last month, he mentioned an idea that he had about writing a collection of poems for the prettiest girls that he knew—poems for girls that have been close to him for a long time, and poems for girls that he has encountered throughout his travels. Knowing many of these girls myself, I fell in love with his idea, because I know that very few others have the ability to capture these girls with such a stripped-down honesty. He's a master at taking what would seem to be moments of breathtaking torment and then exhaling them with a gentle tenderness that any living being would gladly let brush against their cheek like a kiss.

Soon thereafter he began writing his prettiest girl poems, and the finished product, this book that you are holding in your hand is John Dorsey's 63rd book of poems. After reading through it, I can say that it is damn sharp and slices right down to the heart. It is quite possibly his greatest work to date.
So, turn each page as if you're slowly walking across that polished hardwood floor to the center, where a spotlight shines straight down, and the prettiest girl at the dance is waiting with a smile, just for you.

- Victor Clevenger, Carrollton, Missouri, 12-4-20.

The Prettiest Girl in Barstow, California

stares out of an ihop window
as middle-aged truckers
roll in and out of the parking lot
of her heart

she smells like coconut oil
& maple syrup
daydreaming of world peace
while eating a pecan waffle

anyone can make a wildflower sound beautiful
the way wind brushes against her legs
as night settles in next to the highway

but she takes the silence of a cactus blossom
to bed with her every night

& the sky goes dim
when she is behind closed doors

& where she goes
is one of the great mysteries
of the universe.

The Prettiest Girl in Fisherman's Wharf

places her hand on my shoulder
to keep my absent-minded legs
from stepping in front
of an oncoming streetcar

her fingers long and cool
like the summer breeze
remind me that i don't yet
want to die alone
or take the form
of a dying bird

i want to love her
just long enough
for a beer to get warm

just long enough
to mean it.

The Prettiest Girl in Philadelphia, Pennsylvania

had red hair & kind eyes
& wore a backless sundress
in the middle of february

she had a mind as big
as the milky way

& freckles all over her body
that kept me from writing
anything.

The Prettiest Girl in Paddington Square

has jagged teeth
& a thick cockney accent
the only thing
her grandmother ever left her

she wears a locket
with a picture of a dead father
she never even knew
to cover a small tattoo of a rose
along the base of her neck

by day she pours beer
& smiles talking about her boyfriend

& by night
she is the most beautiful
flower in brixton

she is the cry of a barn owl
that once thought it might die alone

her heart tucked away
& dreaming

out of sight
to almost everyone.

The Prettiest Girl in Hastings

has the face & body
of a ravaged lion
& is eighty lbs soaking wet

her bones clinging
to a dirty pair of skinny jeans
for support

as she writes song lyrics
along her arms

she has slept rough
& hidden her inner beauty
under the stars
where nobody
will ever
look.

The Prettiest Girl in Reno, Nevada

worked as a nurse
at the university hospital
more than 80 hours a week

she smelled like a tumbleweed
made of rubber & grease
rolling through a busy strip mall
in the middle of winter

where the hills
had stopped her car
in its tracks
just to hear
her laugh.

The Prettiest Girl in Fort Collins, Colorado

had her head half shaved
to beat the summer heat
& would come to my apartment
just to talk & read me a poem
on a couch that was missing
most of its cushions

surrounded by garbage bags & dirty dishes
in a room that tasted like sweat & inspiration

the spit that came off her lips
when she read
was pure music
that proved that punk rock
wasn't dead.

The Prettiest Girl in Jeanette, Pennsylvania

spent her saturday nights sniffing glue
on a snow-covered hill
behind the blockbuster video
in 1995

flashing my friend kris for $20
to pay her late fees

while time stood still
as her nipples
hardened
in the frost.

The Prettiest Girl in Rock Springs, Wyoming

rents unheated hotel rooms
in the middle
of an ice storm

she tells everyone
that they just need
to tough it out
as she hands them a stack
of unwashed towels

saying that her heart
has seen much colder nights
than this.

The Prettiest Girl in Vancouver

had to come to toledo
to lose her mind

slowly

properly

little bit by little bit

waiting by the maumee river
in an empty room
full of torn up sheet music

she would sing an entire opera
while staring at unpainted walls

her husband gone
child taken to a better home

she would scrub her skin
until it was raw
on the inside

every time she dried her hands
she could feel it all
wash away.

The Prettiest Girl in Pittsburgh, Pennsylvania

hands me a blue stuffed dog
at a carnival

saying it matches my eyes

it's been over thirty years
& still no smile
can measure up to hers

no moonlight was meant
to go on this long
unrequited.

The Prettiest Girl in Sheboygan, Wisconsin

is grilling brats in the snow
in a tattered rick springfield t-shirt
as the school crossing guard
falls & slips
on some ice
next to the local pharmacy

as she dreams of palm trees.

The Prettiest Girl in Toledo, Ohio

used to wear a purple sweater
& buy drinks at the bar
with her father's texas oil money

she had hair on her neck
that she had to get removed by laser
every other thursday
or else she would look
like a delicate werewolf

to her the whole city
felt like a slab of glass
a pitcher of clammy beer

& she would drink just enough
to feel beautiful
& ugly again
in the same night.

The Prettiest Girl in Greensburg, Pennsylvania

reads poetry & carries a skateboard
while walking past the train station

she has fiery red hair
& thinks the world ended in 1994

& who are you
to say that it didn't.

The Prettiest Girl in Brighton

is an aging drag queen
who sits playing with a snag
in her fishnet stockings
while sipping a martini
in the early afternoon

she complains about how
brexit is total rubbish
& that she has nobody
to spend christmas
with anymore

as she picks her cane
up off the bar
before heading outside
to sing to
the birds
in the street.

The Prettiest Girl in Findlay, Ohio

once taught inner city kids
in the heart of chicago

she is a pillar of strength
& so fragile you're almost afraid
to touch her
but still pray she is single

she is a warm kiss
with kind fingers
that run along your back
like piano keys

she is a sunflower
with fire
in her belly
who will always
lead you home.

The Prettiest Girl in Santa Rosa, New Mexico

fries eggs & mexican sausage
& dreams of a man
who will take her
out of this place

beyond the pecos
to another part of history

where she waits
by a stream
for him
to kiss
her hand.

The Prettiest Girl in Capitola, California

had green eyes
like a cat
& a sick mother
in germany

every time we went
to the drive-in
she would say
that we could either
fool around
or watch the movie
like adults

it took at least
fifteen times
before i ever saw
a single frame
of film.

The Prettiest Girl in Kansas City, Missouri

had her high school boyfriend's name
tattooed on her arm
with indian ink

she moved into a basement
in raytown with her
newborn baby

working as a museum security guard
where she stole loose bills
from the donation box

to buy enough whiskey
to put in the baby's bottle
to help her make it
through the night.

The Prettiest Girl in Cleveland, Ohio

never lived long enough
to become a crazy cat lady

she used to laugh
talking to me on the phone

about hipster boys
who would sing 1980s power ballads
outside her apartment door
at all hours
of the day
& night

nobody ever thought a serenade
would become a funeral dirge
quite so quickly

she made a list
of 100 things
to do in the city
before she died

but never managed to
finish it

taken far too soon
she became the one news story
she never got to cover

pierced by her uncle's bullet
in a rust belt trailer park
in the middle of the night

her last words
were like a tree
that fell in the woods

that nobody
would ever get
to hear.

The Prettiest Girl in New Orleans, Louisiana

had blue hair & the body of a cherub
sleeping in a room
separated from the rest of her house
by a threadbare curtain

she painted bowls of fruit
& the curves of her breasts
on canvases left to wilt
in the humidity
at 7 am

as she wandered off
to walk her dog
in the rain.

The Prettiest Girl in Belle, Missouri

works long hours
at the local grocery store

& laughs at the jokes
of boys who aren't
half as smart as she is

her parents died in a fire
when she was young

leaving her with
even younger siblings
& smoke that will never
completely leave her lungs

her youth forever
lost in the flames.

The Prettiest Girl in Dallas, Texas

has strong hands
is comfortable in a dust storm

has hair that is the color of corn
that won't grow here
in winter

her lips are kind
& dry
from kissing
the sun

she knows that sometimes
silence is the only answer
you have to give.

The Prettiest Girl in Harper, Kansas

sleeps in a van
in front of the courthouse
covered in newspapers & political pins
for long lost causes
shivering through the night

the same wind
that used to hug her hips
now just drifts slowly by
without even blowing a kiss
in her direction

she was the sweetheart of 1968
burning her bra
in a thousand dreams
of dying cornfields
as a form of protest

they threw rocks through her windows

& once they learned how to
build a fire in the snow
they shook beatniks
from the trees

with a lit match

& ran her right out of town
into the future.

The Prettiest Girl in Eureka Springs, Arkansas

watches a man talk on his phone
as his girlfriend frowns
in a pizza shop
that smells like imported beer
& true love

& before i can even
open my mouth to speak

she says that if
we're ever on a date
i'd better not be on my phone

but the night is cold
& she's never even heard
of the violent femmes

or looked around the corner
for the music in her own heart

thinking her lips are lovely & kissable
simply because they're attached
to her mouth

it isn't enough

& in a few short hours
she will be looking up
at the stars

wondering why
she is sitting
up in bed
before drifting off
to sleep alone.

The Prettiest Girl in Waterville, Ohio

has an aging dog
whose eyes can only see
into the past

it can barely get around
but is always by her side

she carries a weathered candy land board
that rarely takes her anywhere
she doesn't want to go

she sits in the grass
throwing out an old tennis ball
as the sun goes down
& the lights switch on
in the little league field
beside her house

she can hear the dog's tail
wagging in the dirt
as they listen
for the quiet buzzing of fireflies
swooning madly
in their hearts.

The Prettiest Girl on Venice Blvd

wears soggy blue socks
caked in tar & bad decisions
she smells like marijuana
& chicken wings
before the sun
even comes up

she can see into your future
but can't do anything
to change her past

her lips taste like
every girl you've ever loved
for at least ten minutes every day

she sings about mountains
on lew welch's birthday
& holds back tears
until her tongue catches fire
in the wind.

The Prettiest Girl on Christian Street

never finished the 10th grade
but she could pick the perfect song
on any jukebox
as long as it
had some iggy pop

she was born late for everything
with the sun going down
as she cried
looking at her father
for the first time

not knowing it would be
the last time
she'd ever see him.

The Prettiest Girl in Sandusky, Ohio

had a haircut like a poodle
& two of my oldest friends
chasing after her
all summer long

& all i ever wanted
was a good slice of pie
& an unmade bed to fall into
at the end of the night
without having to
check myself
for fleas.

The Prettiest Girl in Irwin, Pennsylvania

would blast alice cooper & billy idol
as we watched the snow fall
from a covered porch swing in 1984

back then prince
really could make doves cry
just by looking into their eyes

she was a good listener
her weight going back & forth
as she slurped a 64 oz. soda
from the gas station down the street
forever waiting for the sound
of a doorbell
that the local boys
hardly ever rang

she taught me about true joy
but could never find it herself

in those quiet moments
in between screaming
at the top
of her lungs

those few lean seconds
spent trying to convince herself
that it was all
just some
rock n roll fantasy.

The Prettiest Girl in Independence, Missouri

has been drinking
all day & all night
but still looks
as fresh as a mormon daisy
straddling the freeway

as she places my mouth
over each of her breasts
& asks me to join her
in the dirtiest bathroom
on west 23rd street

i listen by the window
as an ambulance roars past us
as if smelling a nearby disaster
right as it's happening

i can hear her heart beating faster
with every second
& all i did
was ask her
her name.

The Prettiest Girl in Muskogee, Oklahoma

is descended from a tribe
with roots that are older
than the castle walls
that sit just off the highway

most days she feels invisible
serving tables of tourists
at a casino that seems so far away
& lonely
in the night sky

pride is a forgotten language here
in a lawless land
without a love story

where most birds would
just simply
fly away
without ever
looking back.

The Prettiest Girl in Columbus, Ohio

has had a thousand lovers
between here & the interstate

she has driven hundreds of miles
in a borrowed van
to sit in my studio drinking beer
next to a space heater
to tell me
about all of them

she stands up while reading my palm
chattering on & on about
our great glorious future
filled with giggling babies
& warm street corners

before turning to leave
offering a kiss
on the lips
in place
of the sun.

The Prettiest Girl in Colfax, California

throws some wood
into her pot belly stove
as we talk about her family
& the revolutionaries
that have come & gone
in these woods
for generations

she makes me a pot of tea
saying she came here
in the summer of love
a young mother with a green thumb
& not much else

offering me a summer job
helping to bring in the harvest

saying that family
is the only thing
you can trust
when things get savage
in the winter frost

saying that even now
she has to be careful
which dreams she lets paw at her heart
& which she leaves behind
in the earth.

The Prettiest Girl in Fraser, Colorado

has deep blue eyes
& can see inside the heart
of a mountain

she is a hawk on fire
a split second in a long life
a roadside miracle with lovely skin
waiting for a slow dance
to lead
her nowhere.

The Prettiest Girl in Wichita, Kansas

has been waiting to die
since she was in high school
with her cheerleader pom poms
& biography of andy warhol
tucked in every suitcase
she's ever packed

she dreams about
putting a cigarette out
on nick cave's arm
the cherry still burning
a golden orange
in the shape
of a rose.

The Prettiest Girl in Austin, Texas

claims to have the best ass
in the city

a perfect apple shape
for roaming hipster bars

this town used to be *so* cool

now she has to drink malt liquor
out of a paper bag
in an empty field

just to stay ahead
of the curve.

The Prettiest Girl in Sacramento, California

is a cool breeze
in an old jeep
that she drives
with the top down

she has had every job there is
for at least a single shift

she knows how to listen
to the rain

& make it laugh

she knows how to make
the whole world
feel loved.

The Prettiest Girl in Yuma, Arizona

makes breakfast at 6 in the morning
with a sizzling skillet

at a time of day
when we are all
weary travelers

but we leave hungrier
than the chinese children
who are filled with knowledge
from the pixels
of her husband's
computer screen.

The Prettiest Girl in Omaha, Nebraska

lives above a gay bar
that seems to pump in house music
around the clock

she has no knobs
on her cabinet doors
& sleeps on the floor
with her cat

humming glenn miller
his melodies from a better time
rocking them both to sleep

on a good night
she dreams that
she is rosie the riveter
filled with pride

& not just some lonely girl
walking up those stairs
to puke in the sink.

The Prettiest Girl in New Canaan, Connecticut

slept with me on a couch
while nursing a bad summer flu

our hearts felt warm
with the fever of youth

wrapped around each other
as she talked about how
she just wanted a comfortable life

i've never been comfortable

& i've never slept through
a single night since then

her voice on the dead end
of every telephone wire

i'd do anything to have her
here with me now

i would happily nod
hold her hand
& not say anything
at all.

The Prettiest Girl in Kingston, New York

can drink you under the table
with her gin & tonics
boiling nathan's hot dogs
at 3 in the morning
because she can't cook
anything else

& you love her
for it

laughing until the sun
comes up

arm in arm

knowing you will always
love her
for it.

❦

About the Author

Photo credit: Milenko Budimir

John Dorsey lived for several years in Toledo, Ohio. He is the author of several collections of poetry, including *Teaching the Dead to Sing: The Outlaw's Prayer* (Rose of Sharon Press, 2006), *Sodomy is a City in New Jersey* (American Mettle Books, 2010), *Tombstone Factory* (Epic Rites Press, 2013), *Appalachian Frankenstein* (GTK Press, 2015), *Being the Fire* (Tangerine Press, 2016), *Shoot the Messenger* (Red Flag Poetry, 2017), *Your Daughter's Country* (Blue Horse Press, 2019), and *Which Way to the River: Selected Poems 2016-2020* (OAC Books, 2020). His work has been nominated for the Pushcart Prize, Best of the Net, and the Stanley Hanks Memorial Poetry Prize. He was the winner of the 2019 Terri Award given out at the Poetry Rendezvous. He may be reached at archerevans@yahoo.com.

www.ingramcontent.com/pod-product-compliance
Lightning Source LLC
Chambersburg PA
CBHW051739040426
42447CB00008B/1211